This Way to the Cross

This Way to the Cross

C. A. ROBERTS

BROADMAN PRESS · Nashville, Tennessee

Second Printing
422–294

DEWEY DECIMAL CLASSIFICATION NUMBER: 248
Library of Congress Catalog Card Number: 66–15147
Printed in the United States of America
3.5O66KSP

to Dolores

who is more a part of the

inspiration and content

of my work

than one would ever dream

Preface

An old man sits on his front porch in a rocking chair. He leans back, closes his eyes, and says: "I believe in 'live and let live.' I don't plan to mix in anybody's business, and I don't want anyone meddling in mine."

In simple, down-to-earth phrases he has expressed his philosophy—his way of life. He may not have thought of it as philosophy, but such it is. It lies behind every action he performs. It molds every attitude he has. It colors every decision he makes.

Technically, the word philosophy means "love of wisdom." More simply, it can be defined as "a way of life." A person's philosophy of life can be a very innocent thing. It can be as deadly as a loaded gun. It can turn the tides of history for good or evil. Men do not move from decision to decision in an objective vacuum. They respond to specific situations out of the general pattern of their way of life.

In the following pages we shall examine certain philosophies which surrounded the cross of Jesus Christ. We shall see that the ways of life which led to the cross are as eternal as human nature. They are as contemporary as tomorrow's newspaper. They are still as forceful for destructive purposes as they were in the first century.

It may be that here you will find the story of your life. I challenge you to examine with an open heart the ways of life which led to the cross. Relive them as though you were there. Better still, relive them as though Christ were on trial today.

Contents

This Way to the Cross

I

The Way of Peter—
COWARDICE

---

*The courage of the enemy and
the cowardice of a friend
helped him die*

MARK 14:27–31, 66–71

What turns a potentially brave man into a coward? What are the roots of cowardice? Is a person born a coward? Does something biological trigger cowardice?

World War II and the Korean War produced an interesting contrast. During World War II many American soldiers were taken as prisoners. However, the enemy simply could not build prison camps that could long contain American boys. No matter how tight the security, no matter how strong the guard, no matter how high the wall, our boys got out! They dug tunnels, cheated sleep, charged walls—but they escaped. Furthermore, few American boys died in prison camps during World War II. And practically none renounced their allegiance to the United States. This was true despite the fact that many endured severe punishment, constant questioning, and starvation.

The Korean War, a few years later, produced a different story. Only a handful of American boys escaped from prison camps. In fact, very few even tried. Also an astonishingly large number of boys died in Korean prison camps. And the thing that shocked America most was the number of young men who renounced their allegiance to the United States. How is this explained? Was the punishment and brainwashing more severe in the Korean War than in World War II? There is no such evidence. What, then, caused so many young men to lose heart in this second war?

Keep in mind that in World War II the lines were clearly drawn. Any young soldier knew that Adolf Hitler was bad and had to be stopped. He knew that Naziism was one of the worst monsters ever to come on the world scene. Also, he could remember Pearl Harbor. The thought of what the Japanese had done inflamed the young soldier with determined allegiance to a cause.

In the Korean War, the American soldier had a difficult time understanding why he was fighting. He could not understand the concept of limited war. Why must he go so far and then stop? Why could he not stamp out the whole thing in quick order?

I am not inferring there was nothing to fight for in the Korean War. I am saying that the issues involved were complex. Consequently, a desire for heroism was not automatically triggered in the American soldier. He did his duty, but when he was caught, he felt no strong obligation to get back into the fight. Finally, under severe brainwashing, he could not always defend positions that were unclear to him.

One thing is clearly pointed out by the above contrast: *If one is to have courage in a crisis, he must have a commitment that is clear and definite in his own mind.*

A Man Called Peter

Every preacher sooner or later explores the paradox of Simon Peter. On the eve of the crucifixion, Peter boldly told the Lord he would die for him (v. 31). An hour later, Peter cut off the ear of a soldier who came for Christ (v. 47). *One hour later,* Peter responded to a question concerning Christ by saying, "I know not this man" (v. 71).

Who was this man of shifting loyalties? Simon Peter was possibly the closest associate Jesus Christ had while he was on earth. He was one of Christ's dearest friends prior to the crucifixion. He was one of his most dedicated followers after the resurrection. Peter was the leader of the apostles. He was never officially appointed to this position. He rather assumed the leadership by coming to the front and being willing to do everything he was called upon to do. Simon was a man of boldness. He grew up around the boat docks. He cut his teeth as a young sailor. He was a man of bravery.

This same man—bold of spirit and a leader of men— helped crucify the best friend he ever had. There was no malice in his action. There was nothing premeditated in his deed. Probably, at the time, Simon could not have explained why he did what he did. The brutally important fact is that he did it. He denied his Lord. The question we seek to answer is, "Why?" In our search for a clue, we shall use the following thesis: deep within Simon's "way of thinking" there was a fatal flaw. In a moment of crisis, this flaw found its way to the surface. It led to an act of spiritual cowardice.

Peter's Early Commitment

What made Simon Peter follow a particular commitment for three years and then surrender to an act of cowardice in one night? I am sure there were many reasons, questions, and impulses which filled his mind. I do not pretend to know them all. I would like to offer one possibility as a part of Simon's dilemma.

Simon Peter became a disciple during the time of Christ's greatest popularity. Early in his ministry, Christ was received with applause and approval. Everywhere he went, the multitudes came out to him. Peter came at a time when it was most respectable to be a follower of Jesus Christ. In fact, disciples of Christ were considered an elite set in the beginning.

During those early days, Jesus warned Simon there would be trying days ahead—days that would test every moral and spiritual fiber within him, but Peter did not listen closely because he was not concerned for the future. He was drawn by the magnetic personality of Jesus Christ. He was charmed by the joy and excitement that surrounded serving Jesus.

That night by the fire, Simon's props were stripped away. All the popularity and approval which surrounded his early commitment vanished. The vast crowds of followers were gone. His fellow disciples were gone. At least Simon made it to the door of the palace. Andrew, James, and Thaddaeus did not. Jerusalem, which had earlier received Christ, now appeared to be against him. Even Rome was a part of the opposition.

The Fatal Flaw

Simon Peter was alone. He did not even have the face of Christ to look upon. He was completely alone at the fire! In that moment, Simon did not want to think what he was thinking or feel what he was feeling. But a flood of doubt came rushing into his mind. He found himself asking, "Can I alone be right and the whole world be wrong?"

It was too great a decision for Peter to make and too inconsistent with his past relationship to Christ. He decided to play it safe. He stood at the fire and said of the best friend he ever had on the earth, "I never knew him."

The Contemporary Scene

Before we condemn Simon too quickly, let me offer an analysis of the contemporary religious condition in our country. I have a feeling the fireside scene of Simon summarizes the greater portion of modern-day Christianity as it faces the world.

We are not presenting a strong Christian witness to our

world. Yes, there is still a reasonable number of Christians tucked safely in church on Sunday morning. There is an even smaller number making a bold and courageous effort at witnessing to the Christian faith. But what about the great bulk of Christianity? What happens to most Christians when they get back into the world on Monday morning? Back into the world of finance? Back into the whirl of social life? Back into the pressure of moral decision? Back into the arena of academics? What happens then?

Most Christians today return to their weekly worlds with a "play-it-safe" philosophy regarding religion. How many Christians do you suppose could give the following testimony? "I used to be dedicated to Christ earlier in life. However, today the commitment is not nearly as strong or meaningful to me."

False Reasoning

What causes a person to make an early commitment to Christ and later drift from that commitment? I know of one very popular reason among college students. I hear it repeatedly. However, I rarely accept it as the real reason for a person's spiritual drift. It goes something like this:

"Early in life when I was young and naïve and things were simple, I committed myself to Jesus Christ, but now I have grown up. I have examined all the alternatives presented by our age of science. I now realize that I can no longer be intellectually honest and cling to my earlier naïve commitment to Jesus Christ."

The above statement is based on one of the biggest falsities ever peddled to thinking people. I am referring to the false but commonly accepted notion that religion is based on *faith* while other "scientific" ideologies are based on *fact*. Someday, I am going to write a book and entitle it *The Faith Presuppositions of Science*. Do you know what I mean by presuppositions? I am referring to certain things that modern science has accepted as true—and yet, these things *cannot be proved!* They have to be accepted *by faith*. You may ask why men of science would accept anything that cannot be proved. The answer is simple. The acceptance of certain propositions by faith is necessary if scientific research is to continue.

Let me name a few faith presuppositions of science: (1) that nature is orderly, (2) that there is an objective reality, (3) that logic (reason) can be trusted as a mental tool, (4) that memory is trustworthy, (5) that human knowledge is a certainty, (6) that the future shall be like the past, (7) that physical matter is primary and mental awareness is secondary, and (8) that higher levels of nature can only be known by analysis of lower levels.

Here is the point I wish to make. The above eight statements sound reasonable. In fact, I accept them all as truth. However, I accept them just as the scientist does— *by faith!* I challenge anyone to *prove* the above eight propositions to be true. Yet, without accepting them, scientific research would have to come to a halt.

All ideologies of life—materialism, naturalism, communism, scientism, existentialism, behaviorism—are based partly on things which cannot be proved. They must be accepted by faith. Whatever the cause for spiritual drift, the reason is rarely intellectual. Doubts and questions usually come in time, but they do not normally mark the beginning of the drift away from a more dedicated allegiance to Christ.

Another Reason

In many instances, the drift away from dedication has to do with the philosophy which gripped Simon Peter. Let me explore the past in the light of Simon's experience.

Possibly you made an early commitment to Jesus Christ during a time of popularity. Those around you were encouraging you to place your trust in Christ. At the time, it seemed as though everybody in *your* world believed in Jesus Christ. On Sunday, the preacher would tell you that in the future it would not be easy to be a Christian. He told you that you would grow up into a world of opposing alternatives. Your moral life would be tested. Your academic life would be tested. Remaining true to Christ would take the best effort you could muster.

But you didn't listen. Oh, you heard, but you didn't really listen. For your faith in the beginning was not simply in Christ alone. To a large degree, your faith was undergirded by the fact that almost everyone around you had faith. Therefore, you assumed that since everyone in your world believed, obviously believing was the thing to do.

Then one day you grew up into a hard, cold world; a

world of high society and easy living; a world of financial give and take; a world where academics were personified and religion was either frowned upon or ignored. Everywhere you turned it seemed that someone was nailing Jesus Christ to a cross. He was being nailed to a cross socially, morally, and academically. Occasionally an angry judge would whirl and ask you of your relationship to Christ. And you would sit in the back of a classroom, or at the desk of a business, or in the corner at some party—and tremblingly reply, "I never knew him."

Why? Because you thought and studied it through intellectually and found serving Christ too naïve and incredible? No! You moved away from your early commitment because it was no longer popular.

Every preacher knows personally what I am talking about. Many are the preachers who start their ministries from a conservative viewpoint, only to become more liberal with each passing year. Is this because the preacher becomes more of an intellectual with the passing of time, and thus finds more loopholes in his faith? I am afraid not. What happens is that a preacher leaves the seminary and spends more time each year in a liberal environment. It is not the logic of thought but the pressure of people that moves him to a more liberal viewpoint.

Let me ask a personal question. Have you moved away, to any degree, from the early dedication you had to Christ? If you have, then let me ask another question. Can you honestly say you have done everything within your understanding to search through and rediscover the revelation of God in Christ? I submit to you that the person who moves away from an early commitment to Christ, *primarily* because it is no longer popular, is a coward.

Had such an individual been present at the crucifixion, he would have helped nail Christ to the cross, just to play it safe.

I Know Him

What caused Simon to weep bitterly shortly after the fireside experience? Was it merely the knowledge that he had failed Christ? No, it was more. Peter had lied! He had said, "I do not know him." For the next thirty years, he spent his life saying, "I know him, I know him." But I daresay he never really got over that one night when he said, "I never knew him."

May I share a personal word at this point? This particular subject has a special meaning to me, for I have a problem similar to Simon's. I want to be intellectually accepted. I am caught up in the tempo of our day. I do not want to be thought of as being naïve. I shrink from this. I want to be accepted as a thinking individual. My problem is basically and simply this: *I know Jesus Christ.*

I do not just mean I have heard about him and know about him. I mean I know Jesus Christ personally in an experience. I grant you this does not free me from the problems of doubt and lack of understanding. In fact, I could say I actually have more questions about religion today than I had fifteen years ago. There are multiple problems which must be battled through in the mind and heart, but this does not alter the fact that I know Jesus Christ.

Let me tell you what I do when doubts and difficulties begin to haunt me. I sit down in my study and let my mind wander back through the years. I go back to a time when my life was overwhelmed with a sense of shame and guilt. My life wasn't going anywhere. I had no purpose, no sense of direction. My life was pure selfishness from top to bottom. Life, in short, was meaningless; it was empty; it was hollow; it was a sham. I would lie down at night and guilt would hover close to me.

Then I would recall hearing of Jesus Christ. I do not mean just the doctrines of the church. I began to hear about Jesus Christ. This One who came to tell the truth about the meaning of life. This One who came to offer life abundantly.

I found myself praying not just in a church service or somewhere with my head bowed for a moment. I entered a period of soul-searching through a process of prayer. I found myself saying, "O, dear God, if there is light that can shine in a darkened heart like my own, if there is direction that can be given to a misdirected life like my own, if there is truth that can replace the bundle of lies on which my life is built, if Jesus Christ can walk into my life and live with me and bring to me this life—then I want it! I want it desperately!"

Something began to happen to me: not in a minute, or an hour, or in one night, or in one church service, but over a process of time light began to come. And the closer I came to the knowledge of Jesus Christ, the more certain I was. Suddenly a sense of joy came into my life. I abandoned myself completely to the cause of Jesus Christ. Little by little a course was set, and I had a direction to my life. I had a goal. All things began to fall in place. A peace of mind and heart began to consume me. I simply must confess that everything Jesus Christ ever said he would do for a person he has done for me. I cannot divorce myself from the experience that Jesus Christ brought to me. I know him.

To those of you who may have drifted, for whatever reason, I call you. Before you surrender yourself to something less, before you give your body, mind, and soul to an alternative that promises more than it can fulfil, I call you. I do not call you back to that same naïve faith you had as a child. I do not call you merely to return to the creed of a church. I call you to stand before Jesus Christ and take a long, searching look. Listen closely to what he said. Look carefully at what he did. Examine openly who he was.

I call you to go and stand one more time at that cross. I call you to fight your way through the senseless mob. Make your way to the One who brought you more of life than you could have found for yourself. Having fought your way through the crowd, look up at him. Say courageously and unashamedly, "I know him. He did not fail me then. I will not fail him now."

II

The Way of Judas—
MATERIALISM

---

*Not by thoughtless acts of
violence, but by the thought-out
philosophies of men
did he die*

MATTHEW 27:1–5

Several years ago the *New York Times* carried a
heartrending story about a London secretary. The young
lady spent the afternoon contemplating a suicidal jump
from a 240-foot high ledge. A minister, Canon Theodore
Milford, talked with her for an hour. At the end of the
hour she jumped. The minister offered the following
explanation. The girl was not intoxicated. She was neither
"out of her mind," nor experiencing hysteria. Very simply,
to her own mind, life had been drained of all its meaning.
And with the loss of meaning also went the will to live.

The Man Judas

Judas was a man who betrayed Jesus Christ for thirty
pieces of silver. Later he took his life: not because he was
"insane," nor because he momentarily lost control of

himself. Judas committed suicide because he had based his life on a certain set of values. In his last hours, he watched those values lead him down a dead-end street. He was left with only one possible alternative which might restore meaning to his life, and that alternative he had helped nail to a tree.

I shall not try to defend Judas, but I would like to take the crime of Judas down off the pinnacle of almost superhuman and unapproachable guilt where we have placed it. I would like to bring his deed down within reach of ordinary people where it belongs. To do this, several things must be said in Judas' behalf.

1. *Judas Iscariot was not a thoroughly evil man.*—When one thinks of a genuinely evil man, he thinks of a Hitler, or an Eichmann, or a Stalin. Judas was none of these. He never committed a single crime that would have placed him in jail for one day in our country. Also bear in mind that for three years Judas was closely associated with the disciples of Christ. During this time he never did a thing that caused the disciples to be suspicious of him. He was not a thoroughly evil man.

2. *The decision to betray Jesus reached a climax in the mind of Judas only twenty-four hours before the deed was performed* (26:14–16).—This was not a plan Judas came to three years earlier, upon becoming a disciple. He had not concealed a plot of sabotage in his mind for two years, waiting to the last moment to spring it. The final decision to betray Christ was made on the eve of the Last Supper.

3. *When Judas committed the act of betrayal, he had no idea this deed would lead to the death of Jesus Christ.*— He was not naïve. He thought the authorities might send Christ from Jerusalem, publicly humiliate him, or even imprison him. But he had not considered that the kiss in the garden would lead to death. This is the only basis on which Judas' action before the elders (27:1–5) can be explained. This is the only satisfactory explanation for his suicide. Judas did not know the magnitude of his deed.

A Two-Hat Philosophy

If the above statements have any credibility—and I am convinced they do—we must answer one significant question. What caused him to do it? What was the trap into which Judas fell during those last few days in Jerusalem —a trap from which there was no escape?

The thing which trapped Judas was his way of life. Let me repeat the idea which I pray will permeate this book. Everybody has a way of life. I have a way of life. You have a way of life. You have certain values by which you live. You do not daily articulate these. Seldom do you stop and say, "These are the things that matter most to me." But they are there. Many times these values are subconscious; they go unnoticed. But they are there, molding your life. As the years go by they come to mean more and more. Finally, when moments of crisis or decision come, your philosophy of life dominates your decisions.

What was Judas' way of life? Simply stated, *Judas Iscariot was a materialist.* In fact, Judas was a paradox, for he wore *two hats*. He wore a *religious* hat and also a *secular* hat. One must concede that Judas was a religious man. He attended synagogue services. He served as a disciple. He supported missionary causes. All this was under his religious hat. Undeniably, Judas was also secular. He had a keen interest in money. He was consistently influenced by power. He was keenly impressed by success. Most of all, he looked out for himself. All this was under his secular (or materialistic) hat.

How did a man with such a dual philosophy ever become a follower of Jesus Christ? The answer is not difficult to discover. There is almost always a secular attraction in any form of organized religion. This was true even in the religious activity that surrounded Jesus Christ. Judas was attracted by such a secular appeal.

There was always plenty to eat when Christ was present. There was also power when Christ was near. Not only were the lame healed, but men also recognized a peculiar authority in Jesus Christ. Obviously, success accompanied Christ, especially during the early days. Crowds came out to meet him in every city. Therefore, from a secular point of view, Judas found it safe to be religious around Christ. He apparently felt he had everything to gain and nothing to lose. He even became the treasurer.

The Winds of Rejection

Everything was all right until that last week, but during those last days, the winds of rejection began to blow. To the mind of Judas, these winds of rejection blew away the power of Jesus. They blew away his success. They blew away the crowds, and the influence, and left Christ stripped and alone.

These same winds also blew off one of Judas' hats. Although Judas had worn two hats, only one dominated his life—the secular. It was his secular hat that stayed on. Judas saw Jerusalem turning against Jesus. He saw the power waning. He saw the success going. Judas saw himself holding an empty bag.

Suddenly he found himself a part of something that was poor, something that was rejected, something that was outcast. All of this was against everything Judas desired about life. In the moment of crisis, his philosophy of materialism dominated his decision. Judas felt he had no choice but to betray his true self or betray Christ.

America Under Two Hats

We must pause in our story. Otherwise we will once again put the crime of Judas beyond our reach. We cannot leave him alone in the commitment of his evil deed. Therefore, we must look for a moment at twentieth-century America. Interestingly enough, you and I live in a country that wears two hats. No one would deny that America is religious. Look at the traffic jams around the churches on Sunday morning. Of course we Americans are religious. We attend religious services, support religious causes, do religious deeds.

However, as Americans, we must also admit that we are

secular. We are keenly interested in money. We are constantly influenced by power. We are supremely impressed by success. Most of all, we look out for ourselves. We are a nation that goes to church on Sunday morning. But what are we Monday through Saturday? What are we in our business lives, social lives, moral lives, and private lives? The truth is that during the week we are a nation that becomes dominated by economic interests, political interests, and the drive for success.

Understand clearly what I am saying. I am not merely stating that there are two separate groups in America—a secular group and a religious group. I am saying the same people who sit in church on Sunday morning enter a different world on Monday morning. The same people who use the language of religion on Sunday, adopt the logic of business, the logic of economics, and the logic of academics the rest of the week. The same people who are religious on Sunday are in turn motivated and dominated by material and secular interests Monday through Saturday.

Your Hats

Do you find the above difficult to believe? Then let me ask you two questions. Do you wear two hats? Let me break it down. Do you consider yourself irreligious? I think not. If you were to answer yes, you would probably do it privately. Now for the other question: look carefully at your business life, school life, social life, and personal life. Would you say that Monday through Saturday the above areas are dominated and motivated by spiritual interests? Or is it possible that just the opposite is true?

If so, then you are a person of two hats. Furthermore, when the winds of economic, social, and moral pressure come, you know which hat blows off—your religious hat! Your secular hat stays on. For although your language on Sunday is *religious,* deep in your heart your philosophy is *material!*

And here is the tragic conclusion of the situation. No matter how religious you pretend to be, if you had been present, you might well have done as Judas did. You say, "Oh, I would never under any circumstances have helped put Jesus Christ to death." Well, I submit to you that Judas would not have either if he had known the magnitude of his deed. This is what is so terrifying about misdirected human beings parading under a false philosophy. We become so insensitive in the scheme of things that we have no understanding of the enormity of our sins against people around us—much less against God himself!

The Fatal Flaw

The story does not end at this point, for there is always a fatal flaw within the person who wears two hats. The flaw was there with Judas. He could rid himself of *it* (his shell of religion), but he could not rid himself of *him!* Judas could rid himself of the religious organization that surrounded Jesus Christ, but he made one mistake: he came to know Jesus Christ too well.

Judas was fed up. He had been looking for a materialistic Messiah. He was convinced that a Messiah would come in great power; that he would set up a military kingdom and perform with the sheer magic of might. And that's how he wanted it. He wanted money in his pocket and magic in his religion. At first, Judas thought Jesus fulfilled all his expectations. Then the organization turned into one of submission before his very eyes. Judas reached the point where he could say, "Hang the submission; hang Galilee; hang the apostles!" Yet down in his heart he kept hearing a voice say, "Yes, *but what about him?*"

Judas reached the point where he could honestly say, "Hang the Sermon on the Mount; hang the bread and the fish; hang the promises about the future!" But something down inside kept saying, "Yes, but *what about him?*" For although Judas could shed the religious organization, he could not say in his heart that he was against Jesus Christ.

The betrayer knew that in Jesus Christ he had found all that he had ever wanted to be in life himself. He knew that everything he had ever come to know about goodness, love, beauty, truth, holiness, and purpose, he had found in Jesus Christ. He didn't know how much all this had meant to him until suddenly he saw the whole thing nailed on a cross. Then he came and said, "O Christ, I did this to you!" And he ran and *cut the head from beneath both hats.*

Your Flaw

Herein is the flaw of any person who wears two hats. Secular influences may have convinced you that you have outgrown your religion. You may think you have become too sophisticated, intellectual, or wealthy to remain "in the fold." You may think you have reached the place where you can shed the religious influences of your past. Possibly you have even reached the point where you resent what happened to you in the past with regard to religion. Maybe you feel you were coerced into accepting things you did not really understand or had not really accepted. Now you can say, "Hang the church back there; hang that preacher; hang that Sunday School." But you see, that is not the point. The real question you must face is, "What about him?"

You might feel like saying, "Hang the things they told me I couldn't do; hang the things they told me I had to do." But that is not the issue. The question is, *What about him?* The issue you must settle is this: Are you certain that you have found enough in a material, secular, critical world of thought to nail that precious life to a cross, and walk away?

Several years ago there was a disturbed young priest at the University of Paris. He came one day to make his confession. He sat down in the booth and began to talk, casually and aimlessly. There was an older and much wiser priest beyond the screen. The older minister realized the boy did not have his mind on what he was saying.

Presently, he interrupted the boy to say, "Young man, you don't mean a thing you are saying, do you?" The boy, at first startled, shot back an answer. "You are right. I don't. And I'll tell you why. I'm fed up with this whole business of religion. It doesn't make a bit of sense to me. I'm fed up with these rules and restrictions; I'm fed up with all this ritualism; I'm fed up with this booth; and I'm fed up with people like you. I want to get out."

The older priest replied, "Then, Son, I think you should. But if you are getting out, make the break clean. Don't simply go half way." He paused a moment and continued. "To show you what I mean, I want you to do one last thing before you go. Will you do it?"

The boy replied, "If I can."

The priest explained his request. "I want you to go across the street to the Cathedral of Notre Dame. I want you to go inside and make your way down to the altar. There you will find the life-size replica of Christ hanging on the cross. I want you to stand there and look up into his face. Then say aloud, 'I did this to you and *I do not care.*'"

The boy said he would do it. He left the building, crossed the street, and entered the cathedral. He made his way down the aisle. He had never been inside the church when it was completely empty. There was no chanting. There was no music. The silence was almost suffocating.

Finally, he found himself standing before the altar. He looked up at the replica of the cross. After an eternal moment, he began, "I did this to you"—but he did not finish. A second time he began, "I did this to you"—and a second time he did not finish. The third time he did not look up. Slowly, he dropped to his knees, bowed his head, and said, "O God, I did this to you, and *I do care!*"

Before we close this chapter on Judas, I am going to ask you to do an ugly thing. I am going to ask you to take everything you know about Jesus Christ—not the church, or the actions of other people—only what you know of Christ. Take everything he ever said, everything he ever did. Take everything he has ever meant to you personally. I want you to take it all and, in your mind, nail it to a cross —all of his truth, all of his goodness and love. I want you to picture yourself nailing all this to a cross. Then, stand there and look into that knowing, loving, caring face and say, "I did this to you." And I hope that having done it, you *will* care.

III

The Way of Caiaphas—
RELIGION

Even the hands of religion
helped in his death
JOHN 18:13–14, 19–23, 28

Prompted by the kiss of Judas, Roman soldiers took Christ to the house of Annas. It is not known why they took him there. Annas was no longer high priest. He had held the position earlier in the year. However, he had released the position to his son-in-law, Caiaphas. The soldiers may have still looked upon Annas as the leader of Judaism. His house may have simply been the closest. He may have been the last one with whom the soldiers had dealt. At any rate, we have no record of any word spoken between Christ and Annas. The Scriptures simply tell us that Annas immediately sent Christ to Caiaphas.

The Position of High Priest

Following the close of Old Testament history, Judaism split into a number of specific groups. There were several minor factions. However, Judaism became predominantly a two-party system, the Sadducees and the Pharisees.

The Pharisees were a conservative group. They were primarily interested in ritualism and ceremonialism. Out of this group came the scribes, who made numerous additions and minute interpretations concerning the law of Judaism. The Sadducees were more liberal than the Pharisees. They dealt mainly in politics under the guise of religion. They were even heretical in some of their doctrines. For instance, they did not accept the doctrine of the resurrection of the dead, or belief in a future life.

These two groups, Pharisees and Sadducees, jointly composed one great governing body for the Jewish nation. Seventy-one members made up the governing council which was called the Sanhedrin. Men such as Gamaliel and Nicodemus were members of the Sanhedrin. The high priest was chairman of the Sanhedrin. He was recognized as the top man of the nation by the Jews. He was also recognized as the top man among the Jews as far as Rome was concerned. Rome only recognized one man regarding internation legal matters. That one man was the high priest. Caiaphas was, therefore, the proper man to see regarding the Jewish problem involving Jesus Christ.

An Illegal Trial

The procedure by which Jesus Christ was tried was illegal in many ways. Under Jewish law, a trial could not begin after dark. A person could not be executed on the same day sentence was passed. A person could not be sentenced on a feast day, or the day before a feast day. A person could not be sentenced on a sabbath, or the day before a sabbath. All these laws were set aside when Jesus Christ was tried, sentenced, and executed. The council was determined in this instance that nothing should stop them. Messengers were hastily sent out (apparently to a select portion) asking the Sanhedrin to gather at the palace of Caiaphas.

There was another interesting and significant illegality about the trial of Christ. For forty years previous to this occasion, the members of the Sanhedrin had not passed on matters leading to capital punishment. They had decided it was their place to save life, not destroy it. This precedent was altered the night Jesus Christ was tried.

One more fact is important to the night's proceedings. Even if the entire council had been determined to put Jesus to death, one man could have stopped it—the high priest. As chairman of the Sanhedrin, he could have dismissed the trial, or at least postponed it. Instead, it was Caiaphas who pressed the issue. The Scriptures tell us it was Caiaphas who first put into words that it was going to be necessary to put Christ to death (John 11:49-50).

The High Priest's Philosophy

By what reasoning could a man of such high religious stature pass a sentence of death upon Jesus Christ? There is no question that Caiaphas was a devoted religious man. Time and space do not permit a detailing of the demands made upon a high priest. It was necessary for him to have a background of religious dedication. He was submitted to numerous sacrifices and disciplines which were permitted to the ordinary man. Caiaphas was, indeed, a religious man. Yet, *because* of his religion, and not *despite* it, Caiaphas helped seal the death of Jesus Christ.

His reasoning was very simple. Caiaphas carefully and logically reasoned to himself as follows: (1) I am *religious* (in fact the head of his religion), therefore I am *right*. (2) If I am right, then Jesus Christ is wrong. (3) If Jesus Christ is wrong, then he is guilty of blasphemy and must be put to death.

A Strange Fact

It is easy to see that if the initial premise of Caiaphas was false, then his whole logic was wrong. And his premise was that *he was religious, and, therefore, he was right*. But even so, it is hard to conceive of a man of high religious position passing such a harsh sentence as death. It seems that his heart would have been tempered with compassion.

At this point a strange fact emerges. Would it surprise you to realize that, while Christ was on the earth, the bitterest adversaries he faced came from the ranks of religion? The harshest treatment and fiercest opposition Christ received during his ministry came from people who acted in the name of religion.

There is a problem of reversed order which needs to be mentioned here. When we seek to interpret the New Testament, there is an area of emphasis which we often reverse. For instance, when we seek to categorize sins, we invariably begin with sins of the flesh. We enumerate sins

of social crime, vice, and immorality. These can be more
easily observed by society. We leave sins of the mind,
heart, and spirit to the last.

This was not the order of emphasis of Jesus Christ. I
challenge you to try an experiment. Take your New
Testament and underline every instance when Jesus
Christ raised his voice strongly against people who were
guilty of sins of the flesh. He did not condone such sins.
He definitely spoke against the sins of the flesh, but
always out of a heart of compassion. Christ had great
sympathy for a man who was trapped by a physical habit
or caught in a period of vice. When *did* Christ raise his
voice and use the severest language at his disposal? He
did it when speaking of men guilty of sins of the mind and
spirit. His strongest condemnation was directed against
men guilty of sins of the spirit, committed *in the name of
religion!*

Why was the Sanhedrin up in arms about Jesus? What
made them so mad? The answer is given in the closing
chapters of the Gospels. He spent the last four days of his
life going through the streets of Jerusalem and speaking
against the sins of the Sadducees and Pharisees. Listen to
some of the things he had to say against the leaders of
religion!

Woe unto you, scribes and Pharisees, hypocrites! for ye shut
up the kingdom of heaven against men: for ye neither go in
yourselves, neither suffer ye them that are entering to go in.
Woe unto you, scribes and Pharisees, hypocrites! for ye de-
vour widows' houses. and for a pretence make long prayer:

therefore ye shall receive the greater damnation. Woe unto you, scribes and Pharisees, hypocrites! for ye compass sea and land to make one proselyte, and when he is made, ye make him twofold more the child of hell than yourselves.

Woe unto you, ye blind guides, which say, Whosoever shall swear by the temple, it is nothing; but whosoever shall swear by the gold of the temple, he is a debtor! Ye fools and blind: for whether is greater, the gold, or the temple that sanctifieth the gold?

· · · · · · · · · · · · · · · · · · · ·

Woe unto you, scribes and Pharisees, hypocrites! for ye pay tithe of mint and anise and cummin, and have omitted the weightier matters of the law, judgment, mercy, and faith: these ought ye to have done, and not to leave the other undone. Ye blind guides, which strain at a gnat, and swallow a camel.

Woe unto you, scribes and Pharisees, hypocrites! for ye make clean the outside of the cup and of the platter, but within they are full of extortion and excess. Thou blind Pharisee, cleanse first that which is within the cup and platter, that the outside of them may be clean also.

Woe unto you, scribes and Pharisees, hypocrites! for ye are like unto whited sepulchres, which indeed appear beautiful outward, but are within full of dead men's bones, and of all uncleanness. Even so ye also outwardly appear righteous unto men, but within ye are full of hypocrisy and iniquity.

Woe unto you, scribes and Pharisees, hypocrites! because ye build the tombs of the prophets, and garnish the sepulchers of the righteous, and say, If we had been in the days of our fathers, we would not have been partakers with them in the blood of the prophets. Wherefore ye be witnesses unto yourselves, that ye are the children of them which killed the prophets (Matt. 23:13–31).

Little wonder these men rose up against Jesus Christ. He spent the last four days of his life walking up and down the streets of Jerusalem, saying, *"Caiaphas, you are religious, but you are wrong!"*

The Source of Caiaphas' Religion

How could a man like Caiaphas be so religious, and yet so wrong? How could he rise to the pinnacle of religious achievement and his mind be so completely closed? It was not a requirement of the Sanhedrin that a man have a closed mind. Gamaliel did not have a closed mind. Nicodemus did not have a closed mind. He was a man with many questions. Therefore, he went straight to Christ and unbarred his mind. He began by saying, "Rabbi, we know that thou art a teacher come from God: for no man can do these miracles that thou doest, except God be with him" (John 3:2).

But Caiaphas was a man with a completely closed mind regarding religion. How could this happen? One need only ask one question: *Where did Caiaphas get his religion?* Did he get his religion by searching the word of God? One day Jesus said, "Search the scriptures; for in them ye think ye have eternal life: and they are they which testify of me" (5:39). Did Caiaphas even one time seek out and question Christ personally and sincerely, as did Nicodemus? Did he come to his religion in a spirit of prayer and openness?

The fact of the matter is that Caiaphas got his religion primarily from one source. *He got it from his father-in-*

law, Annas. Obviously, to Caiaphas this appeared to be a valid source. Annas was the high priest—the supreme voice of religion in Jerusalem. But the record also reveals that Annas was something else. He was one of the cruelest, craftiest, most vicious high priests that ever reigned over Jerusalem. It might be said he was 98 per cent politician and 2 per cent religious; yet he operated under the guise of religion. And Caiaphas accepted all of Annas' attitudes in the name of religion. There were many reasons that would prompt Caiaphas to accept such a source. First, Annas was his father-in-law. Second, Annas was high priest. Third, Caiaphas wanted to be high priest himself someday. Therefore, Caiaphas accepted his father-in-law's philosophy of religion without question.

What else, then, could Caiaphas do when he stood face to face with Christ? He had no alternate basis on which to operate. He really had no commitment to God at all. His commitment was to religion with a capital "R." And that religion did not come from God. It came from Caiaphas' father-in-law.

That Thursday night Caiaphas had an opportunity offered to but a few men in history. He could have made *one* decision with regard to *one* man and saved the Jewish nation. Instead, he chose to kill that nation's most beloved Son. And he did it in the name of religion.

What Is Your Source?

It sounds too incredible to be true, that a man could be so religious and at the same time so misguided. But let me ask you a personal question. How much of your religion is secondhand? How many of your own beliefs can you say you came to through a search of your own? You searched the Scriptures. You sought the council of many men wiser than yourself. You examined alternatives on numerous points of personal conviction. After long and prayerful inquiry you came to the best ground on which you felt a person could stand religiously. Is this the honest appraisal of your religious convictions?

Or might it be said that, in part, your case is similar to that of Caiaphas? You came to most of your religious attitudes by a process of hand-me-downs. You simply borrowed from your parents or other people closest to you. You merely blindly accepted your heritage. You made the same assumption Caiaphas made. You assumed that the viewpoints closest to you were automatically right.

Let me offer some particulars for sake of clarification. Why are you a member of the particular denomination with which you identify yourself? Why is it that you have passionate and almost violent convictions regarding certain moral and social issues, yet casually dismiss others as unimportant? How did you become so sensitive in certain areas and so indifferent in others?

Take another case in point. We are living in an age when the newspapers daily speak of race revolution. Where did you get the particular attitude you have with regard to people of other races?

Examine for a moment another area. Most of us grew

up amidst tension between Catholics and Protestants. If
you are a Protestant, how did you develop a distaste or
suspicion for those of the Catholic faith? If you are a
Catholic, how did you come to your attitude toward those
of Protestant faith? In all honesty, might you have to
admit that a great many things in your life of religious
interest you did *not* come by through an individual search
of your own? Instead, you have chosen the "religion" of
your heritage. You have chosen those attitudes to which
you were exposed in the ordinary course of life. To a large
extent you have assumed that what was closest was right.

My Past

I do not know about you, but this scares me. I mean
with regard to myself. I have taken a look at my own life.
I must admit that, in large measure, I am a part of my
past. For instance, I am presently serving as the pastor of
a Baptist church. How did I come to this particular area
of service in life? I would like to be able to say it was
reached through careful and prayerful choosing on my
part, and to a large degree I think this is the honest truth.
And yet, this is not the whole story, for I am also an
inseparable part of my past.

Let me illustrate.

I was born in a home of Baptist parents. All of my close
relatives were Baptists. As a child, I went to Sunday
School with Baptist children. In my teens, I was influenced by Baptist preachers. Upon leaving high school, I
felt led of God to enter the ministry. I attended a Baptist

college. After graduating from college, I attended a
Baptist seminary. A Baptist church in Altus, Oklahoma,
then called me as its minister. Later, a Baptist church in
Tallahassee, Florida, began looking among other Baptist
churches for a pastor. Hence, I came to Tallahassee.

I do not feel that I came blindly and thoughtlessly to
my present vocation in life. Yet, there are some questions
I must ask myself in all honesty. What if I had been born
in Boston, Massachusetts, instead of Waco, Texas? What
if I had grown up in an Episcopal home instead of a
Baptist home? What if I had attended Harvard instead of
Baylor? Would I still have been a Baptist preacher? I
think not.

What does this mean? I'll tell you what it does not
mean. It does not mean I must reject everything about
my past, because I have not. It does not mean I must
conclude that everything my parents taught me was
wrong, because I do not. It does not mean I must turn my
back on everything from those people nearest me.

But I'll tell you what else it does not mean. It does not
mean I must accept, without question, everything I ever
heard as I grew up. In fact, I can't afford to, and for good
reason. You and I are living in a new day. We are living in
a day that is both unique and complex. We are living
through an era that demands the freshest insight we can
gather. All around us there are confused alternatives
between which we must choose. Daily we are faced with
the problem of being for certain things without being for
certain other very similar things.

In an age such as ours, I want to be as open and honest as I know how. In this endeavor, I refuse to be strapped to a secondhand religion. Instead, I am going to try and live one day at a time and meet each new problem as openly as possible. As I meet each new situation in life I am going to seek the answer to one question: in this one particular instance, what would Jesus Christ do, or what would he expect me to do? Then I am going to my Bible, get alone in prayer, and stay there until I get the mind of God.

My commitment is not to a church, not to a particular denomination, not to a predetermined viewpoint; my commitment is to God alone. I refuse to pass up an allegiance to Christ, which I feel in my heart, simply in the name of the old-time religion.

The old-time religion is not good enough for me. It may be good enough for you, but it's not good enough for me. It may have been good for my father and mother, and their fathers and mothers, but this is a new day. This is the second half of the twentieth century. There never has been a day just exactly like our day in the history of the world. We are living through a scientific, moral, and social revolution. No other age has ever tried to hold outer space and the crowded community in two frail hands.

Therefore, I don't care what "they" did in the tenth, the fifteenth, or the nineteenth century. I don't care what happened one hundred years ago. The only thing that matters to me is, What does God expect me to do as a witness to Jesus Christ *in America in my age?* That's all that counts.

Therefore, I call you to do a most difficult thing. I call you to find those attitudes in your life that are purely secondhand—unquestioned and untested. I call you to divorce yourself from a mere philosophy of religion, and make sure you are a follower of Jesus Christ and no one else. And, believe me, I know just how difficult a thing this is to do. Our day struggles against it because we are all bound together with *things as they are and always have been.*

The Old Men Who Knew

Several years ago, a parable came across my desk. It was the story of a community settled on a plateau, amidst fertile fields and at the foot of a mountain stream. One day a young boy wandered up a path by the mountain stream. For several days he was not seen. Finally, he returned breathlessly to tell of a richer plateau higher up the mountain.

This presented a problem. The community was governed by a group called "the old men who knew." These men *knew* there was no better plateau than where they were. They told the boy to be silent lest he upset the whole community. But the boy could not be silent for he had seen the higher plateau with his own eyes. The old men who knew were left with no choice. They took the boy to the center of the village and stoned him to death.

The years passed and the fields became barren. The community was going to have to seek a new home. Someone remembered the tale of the young boy years before. A group of young men were sent out and they found the richer plateau. The community moved of *necessity* to higher ground.

More years passed, and one day another boy wandered up a mountain path. He returned to tell of a still richer plateau higher up the mountain. But there was one problem. The young men who earlier moved the community had now become "the old men who knew." They took the boy to the center of the village and stoned him to death.

Take that story and place it beside what Caiaphas did in the name of religion. You will find that the most painful, the loneliest, and sometimes the most dangerous thing a person can do is to try to stand apart from his past —or even his present!

To try to stand alone before God and your own conscience, to try to search out the spirit of Christ and the mind of God is painful, lonely, and dangerous indeed. But, my friend, you must try. For the person who goes through life with an untested, secondhand religion stands the chance of someday being as wrong as Caiaphas. And that person also runs the risk of someday unknowingly or unwantingly nailing an innocent man to a cross—even in the name of religion.

IV

The Way of Pilate—
AMBITION

*In the same breath
he declared Christ innocent
and consented to his death*
MATTHEW 27:1–2, 11–18, 22–26

The members of the Sanhedrin could recommend a death sentence, but they could not carry it out. Any decision of capital punishment had to be both rendered and carried out by Roman authorities. This was the way Rome kept things in hand. It was not enough that Christ be found guilty of the religious charge of blasphemy by the Sanhedrin. It was also necessary that he be taken to the Roman governor and there be tried. Therefore, they took Christ from the palace of Caiaphas to Pilate, governor of Rome in Judea.

The Jewish authorities were faced with a problem as they approached the Roman court. They had to find a charge that Pilate would consider. He would not be concerned one instant with the religious charge of blasphemy. The only charge that Pilate would listen to would have to have a direct bearing upon Rome. Therefore, the

Jewish authorities added one more lie to their scheme. They told Pilate that Christ was guilty of treason against Rome, that he was a revolutionary, that he was inciting an insurrection against the emperor, that he was seeking to establish a separate kingship that would overthrow local Roman rule (Luke 23:2-5).

Pontius Pilate remained as the last legal link between Christ and crucifixion. What transpired before the Roman governor remains as one of the most paradoxical situations ever devised by the human personality. To understand the happenings more clearly, two significant facts should be kept in mind concerning Pilate.

The Paradox

It was no secret that Pilate had an intense dislike for the Jewish religious authorities. In fact, his dislike bordered on contempt. Every opportunity he had, Pilate flaunted himself before the Jews. Other Roman procurators had honored the fact that the Jews did not believe in images. This they did by removing the eagle from their standards —the image of the emperor. When Pilate assumed his duties in Jerusalem, he left the images of the emperor in full display. Pilate also showed his contempt for the Jewish religionists during a water shortage. The town needed an aqueduct and Pilate built it. However, instead of financing the construction with Roman money, he went to the Temple and seized Jewish funds. At every opportunity Pilate displayed his disapproval and distaste for the Jewish authorities.

A second fact should be placed beside Pilate's contempt for the Jews. During the process of listening to charges, and then interviewing Jesus both publicly and privately, Pilate came to the unmistakable conclusion *that Christ was innocent.*

This is not to infer that Pilate was a warmhearted man. He wasn't. Nor does it infer that he had a personal interest in Jesus Christ. He didn't. He probably had never met Christ, though quite likely he had heard of him. But he knew that Christ was not guilty of the charges being made. He knew Jesus Christ was not a revolutionary. He knew Christ was not trying to incite an insurrection against Rome. He knew Christ was not trying to establish an earthly kingdom in competition with the emperor. In fact, he went beyond that. He knew Christ was not guilty of anything. He knew he was a just and good man.

Pilate was a reckless man, and extremely shrewd. Several times he had allowed bloodshed to enhance his own position. But Pilate was not an *oppressive* man. He was not a cruel man. In fact, on that Thursday night Pilate showed Christ respect, pity, and even tenderness. No other ruler ever dealt with Christ half as conscientiously or half as tenderly as did Pilate. Throughout the entire ordeal of the trials even, Pilate was the only witness in Christ's defense. He did everything he could to avoid the inevitable conclusion he could see developing. First, Pilate let Christ speak in his own behalf. Second, he examined Christ privately. Third, he sent Christ to Herod, the governor of Galilee. Fourth, he told the people he found no fault in Christ. Fifth, he announced that Herod found no fault in Christ.

Sixth, Pilate called Christ a just man. Seventh, he stood with Christ on the balcony and said, "Behold the man!" (John 19:5). Eighth, he sought to release Christ outright. Ninth, he tried to substitute Barabbas, a notorious revolutionary, for Christ. Tenth, he had Christ scourged in an attempt to evoke sympathy from the Jews. Eleventh, he brought out a bowl, washed his hands, and announced that he wanted no part in the personal guilt in what was being done to Christ.

Then came the crushing blow, and herein is the paradox. Pilate stood and said, "I declare this man innocent." Then *in the same breath,* he said, *"Take him and crucify him!"* You figure that out. Here was a man who stood before a group of Jewish authorities he literally despised; he also stood before a man he knew was innocent; and, with all the power of Rome in his grasp, he said, "I find no fault in him. Take him and crucify him."

The Philosophy of Pilate

How can these diverse actions of Pilate possibly be explained? For the answer we must look at the philosophy of life by which Pilate had lived for a number of years, a philosophy called *ambition*. Pilate had slowly worked his way up through the military ranks to the position of governor. By his way of thinking, Pilate had said to himself: As I go through life, I will enter into any compromises; I will make any bargains; I will do whatever necessary to achieve the ultimate goals I desire for myself.

This Pilate had done. And along the way, he performed some very rash deeds. In some instances he had over-stepped the bounds even of a Roman governor! No one deed in itself and by itself would be enough to hurt him. But, if all his misdeeds were compiled in full and placed in the hands of his Roman superiors, that could prove to be a most damaging event.

Pilate had never seriously worried about his past, for his philosophy of ambition had never been contested. It had never been brought to a point of conflict—to a showdown. Therefore, the governor didn't realize the trap he had set for himself until that night. But on that fateful night, Pilate was met head-on with a dilemma. The Pharisees and Sadducees were hated of Pilate. But there was something else about them. *They knew Pilate.* They knew his compromises. They knew his bargains. They knew all his rash deeds.

They knew! Not only that, Pilate knew they knew. Even more, they knew that Pilate knew they knew. Further-more, Pilate could tell that these Jews were going to stop at absolutely nothing; he could also tell that they were daring him not to co-operate. In short, Pilate was a man rendered helpless by his past. In the struggle for the top, he had plunged in too deep.

Pilate had gone too far in the past to be able to ignore his past. He was left with two choices: he could do what he knew in his heart was right and take the risk of destroying his career, or he could do what he knew was wrong and escape immediate and personal danger. He chose the latter.

Contemporary Ambition

You might say, "How could a man in Pilate's position reach such a decision? Granted, the Jews knew a little dirt about him. But after all, he was the governor! He had the power of Rome at his disposal. How could the Roman procurator, in the face of a people he despised, tell an innocent man he had to die? How could he do it?"

Let me ask you. How often in your life have conscience, right, and duty pointed you in one direction, and your own personal interests and ambition pointed in another? And, in such instances, how often have you washed your hands of conscience and right and chosen the wrong? Oh, yes, you did just as Pilate. You wavered, debated, and argued. You listened to others, wrung your hands, and hesitated. But finally, when the decision was made, you were swept by the winds of self-interest in the wrong direction.

You might argue that Pilate's case was different. He was standing before Jesus Christ. You might say, "If I had possessed Pilate's power, and the facts I have about Jesus Christ, I would have made a different choice."

Would you have chosen differently if you also had possessed Pilate's past? For remember this one thing: when Pilate stood there that night, his slate was not clean. He was not a knight in shining armor. He stood there with a precarious past record. This was his third strike! One more mistake and he would be out and the Jews knew it.

Let me bring this scene up to date. Suppose Jesus Christ were standing to your right this very moment, and, in all his majesty, that he was asking someone to take the stand in his behalf and declare him innocent—declare him righteous. Next, put yourself in Pilate's position. You have all his power at your disposal; you also have a choice similar to his to make. Change one thing. Let us say you have your own past.

Next, suppose that to your left, instead of a group of angry Jews, there stands everyone who knows the truth about you. People who know you as you really are. People who know your compromises, your secrets, your mistakes and rash deeds. And let us suppose these people are daring you to take a stand for Jesus Christ, daring you to defy them—people who are going to stop at nothing to get what they desire. The choice is yours, and you must make it openly. Let us see how long it will take for your personal interests to close your lips!

It happens every day. We do it in so many minor ways that we do not even realize we are doing it. Recently, I had a man come to me with regard to an election in our city, a man who himself was in politics. He said, "Preacher, I only have one alternative in the coming election. In order to protect my own business and political future, I must cast my *private vote* in one direction, and my *public sentiment* in the opposite direction."

That, my friend, is the very philosophy that helped

crucify Jesus Christ. Pilate took Christ into a room privately, away from the ear of the Jews. In that privacy he said, "Listen to me, you are innocent and I know it. There is something about you I admire and respect. I wish I had more time to know you better. I believe you are a just man." He cast his *private vote* in Christ's direction. Then, he walked back on the balcony, joined hands with *public sentiment,* and sealed the doom of the greatest crime in history.

Jesus Christ still gets crucified in this manner everyday. It does not make a bit of difference what you think about him in private. It does not matter at all what you think of right and good and truth away from the public eye. What matters is what you think openly, when those who defy you are demanding that you do an opposite thing, and the stand you take for what you know to be right.

Too Little and Too Late

Pilate didn't make his decision because he thought it was an *easy* way out. He came to the decision to crucify Christ because he thought it was his *only* way out! And he hadn't made his choice five minutes before he regretted it. Pilate followed the crowd to the place where soldiers were preparing for the execution. It was customary to place an inscription above the head of a criminal defining the nature of his crime. The inscription would be written in the prisoner's native tongue.

The governor took a board and wrote on it the title, JESUS OF NAZARETH THE KING OF THE JEWS (John 19:19).

When the chief priests saw the inscription, they went to
Pilate in a rage. They pointed out his glaring mistake.
"Then said the chief priests of the Jews to Pilate, Write
not, The King of the Jews; but that he said, I am the King
of the Jews" (v. 21).

Pilate replied, "What I have written I have written" (v.
22). He made them know the inscription would remain
exactly as it was. Furthermore, he had it put, not only in
Hebrew, but also in Latin and Greek. He wanted the
world to know that this was the King of the Jews.

Admirable gesture on Pilate's part? Not at all! Because
it was *too little*, and *too late*. And Pilate's case is not
unique. As a pastor, I have repeatedly watched men—
good men—literally prostitute their Christian convictions
in the name of self-interest and ambition. Then I have
watched them later return and perform some meager
religious charity to show their hearts were in the right
place. I have wanted to shout, "Too little, and too late!"

No man is exempt from the pressures of personal
interest and ambition. If you are not careful, you can
spend your entire life doing minor deeds for God that cost
you nothing, only to remain in the shadows when Christ
needs you most. Then someday the books will be closed,
and the only thing written in your record with regard to
Jesus Christ will be, "Too little, and too late!

The Tragic Irony

Here is the trick that life plays. Life always seems to
have a joker for the man who plays it safe. In Pilate's case

the joker was that he thought, in releasing Christ to be crucified, he was escaping all risk—that he was passing up danger. In reality, the thing he passed up was the chance to salute the only real King he ever knew, because they got him—the Jews, that is. A few years later, a minor incident occurred in Samaria. Pilate sent soldiers to put down the uprising. In the process, the soldiers got a little too rough and some Jews were injured. The Jewish authorities reported the happenings to the emperor, Tiberias. Tiberias immediately called Pilate to Rome to stand trial. While Pilate was en route to Rome, Tiberias died. Therefore, Pilate never had to stand trial, but was exiled to the region of the Swiss Alps.

Even today as you travel through Switzerland, you can view a mountain which is called Pilate's mountain. At this point legend tells us far more than we dare believe. Tradition tells us that Pilate never got away from his experience with Jesus Christ. Legend says that Pilate would walk each evening by the lake at the foot of the mountain. As he walked he would look as though he were waiting for someone, as though at any moment that same just man might return. At this time Pilate would wash his hands once again, and return to sleep and try to forget.

From the account of tradition we can sift this much: this man, who made a wrong choice to protect himself, spent his last years *at least* in trouble and remorse; and at most, in insanity and suicide. Of one thing we can be certain: by defending Jesus Christ, Pilate could not have lost more than he otherwise did. For through his wrong choice, the governor of Judea not only lost his job, but also his self-respect.

The Final Question

The first century is gone. This is the twentieth century. The real question is not, "What would you have done had you been Pilate?" That is purely theoretical. The question you must face is the same question Pilate asked, "What shall I do with Jesus which is called the Christ?"

No one holds the answer to this question but you. Maybe you have gone too far. Maybe you have waited too long. Maybe you are already in too deep. Maybe, in the name of ambition and self-interest, you have already sacrificed the last ounce of moral and spiritual integrity you will ever have on this earth. But *maybe you have not.* I can assure you of this: if you have gone too far, nothing you do to protect yourself will keep the bottom of life from someday crumbling beneath your feet. One of these days, in some minor way, life will get you.

There still may be hope for you to make a clean break, and be right. You will never know unless you try. The only way you will know is to be willing to come out in the open. Stand courageously before those who know you and would defy you. Turn and face the righteousness, the truth, and the goodness of Jesus Christ—and salute! If you dare, it may seem too little and too late for those around you who would ruin you if they could. But I promise you, in the eyes of God, it will *be enough;* and *it will be in time.*

V

The Way of the Multitude—
SILENCE

*Not only by the evil of the bad
but by the silence of the good
did he die*

MATTHEW 21:8–11; ACTS 4:1–21

The two higher voices had spoken. Caiaphas, representing the pinnacle of Jewish religious authority, had recommended that Jesus die. Pilate, the supreme voice of Rome in Judea, had consented. The die was cast. We would assume there was no higher court of appeal. Jerusalem and Rome had officially and mutually consented to the crucifixion of Christ. Surely the trial and execution had reached a point of no return.

But there was still one higher court of appeal. It was not an official body, but nonetheless a powerful one. It was a court to which both Jerusalem and Rome had listened in the past. It was a court to which they would listen in the future. It was the court of the people. It was the court of public sentiment.

Jesus Christ did not die in private. He was tried and executed in the city of Jerusalem at feast time. He died in

49

the presence of great crowds of people—people who played a far greater role in his death than they realized. Strangely enough, many of these people participated in the crucifixion of Christ, not by what they did, but by what they failed to do.

In previous chapters we have looked at men who said and did hurtful things during the trial and crucifixion of Christ. In this chapter we will look at those who said and did nothing. Frankly, the silence of the multitude is one of the most puzzling enigmas which came out of the entire ordeal of the cross. To understand the significance of this silence we must examine two factors: the *popularity of Christ*, and the *power of public sentiment*.

The Popularity of Christ

Jesus Christ was popular with the multitudes throughout his entire ministry. The conflict, opposition, and rejection of the third year came from Jewish religious authorities. It did not stem from the multitudes. The popularity of Christ was not confined to a particular area geographically. "There followed him great multitudes of people from Galilee, and from Decapolis, and from Jerusalem, and from Judea, and from beyond Jordan" (Matt. 4:25).

Neither was the popularity of Christ confined to a certain period—at least as far as the multitudes were concerned. The week before he entered Jerusalem for the last time, the following scene took place in Bethany. "The common people therefore of the Jews learned that he was

there: and they came, not for Jesus' sake only, but that
they might see Lazarus also, whom he had raised from the
dead (John 12:9, ASV). When Christ entered Jerusalem
that last week, the following scene took place. "A very
great multitude spread their garments in the way; others
cut down branches from the trees, and strawed [strewed]
them in the way. And the multitudes that went before,
and that followed, cried, saying, Hosanna to the son of
David: Blessed is he that cometh in the name of the Lord;
Hosanna in the highest. And when he was come into
Jerusalem, all the city was moved, saying, Who is this?
And the multitude said, This is Jesus the prophet of
Nazareth of Galilee" (Matt. 21:8–11).

Jesus Christ gained a popularity with the multitudes
early in his ministry, and he never lost it. He didn't lose it
in the second year or the third. He didn't lose it the last
week of his life. Jesus Christ remained popular with the
common people.

Several factors contributed to Christ's popularity. First,
people were drawn to Christ by his *compassion*. When
Jesus Christ came into the world of Palestine, he found an
open sore. We do not see this so much in our own country.
We have a way of taking our diseased and suffering
people and tucking them away in places of rest and care.
At least we hide them in shacks of poverty. However, in
many parts of our world today—in the Orient, India, the
Middle East—diseased and suffering humanity is still on
the streets to be seen. Jesus found the world this way and
had compassion. He spent a great deal of time healing,

encouraging people in their suffering, doing everything he could to help. His compassion reached the multitude.

Second, Jesus was popular with the multitudes because of his *teachings*. When Jesus taught, he had a way of stripping away the legalism from the law. His teachings brought life, encouragement, and hope to his hearers. The simplicity and authority of his words struck home to the hearts of men. Third, Jesus was popular because of the *effect his personality had upon the common man*. He had a way of taking common things and giving them an uncommon value. The men who became the apostles of Christ were common men. They were common business-men, fishermen, and farmers. Yet, they took an uncommon place in history because of the transforming power of the person of Christ.

Not just in the first year of his ministry, but also in the last week of his life, Jesus Christ had more friends than enemies. Some have questioned: "How could it be that the people of Jerusalem cried, 'Hosanna, Hosanna,' the first of the week, and 'crucify him,' the last?" The fact is, these were two different groups. At the first of the week, the whole town gladly came out to meet Jesus. That last night, the chief priests had to search for people who would bear false witness against Christ. The Scriptures indicate they finally found *two* (Matt. 26:60).

Most of the noise at the trial of Jesus was made by the chief priests, scribes, and elders (27:41). They created the appearance of a mob uprising with planted agitators (v. 20). You can underline one fact: that Friday Jesus

Christ was led out to be crucified, he was surrounded by far more friends than enemies.

The Power of Public Sentiment

The question might be raised, "If the multitudes had risen up openly in Christ's behalf that last evening, could it have altered the turn of events?" You can open your Bible and repeatedly find passages that indicate such action had altered proceedings prior to that night. Often the Pharisees wanted to do a certain thing to Jesus Christ, but didn't because they feared the people. Caiaphas was not concerned about Pilate. He had the governor on the spot. However, he was concerned about the people. The whole affair of the trial was planned quickly, and at night, to avoid as many of the common people as possible.

An interesting event is revealed in the fourth chapter of Acts. The scene was eight weeks after the crucifixion. Peter and John were brought before Caiaphas for preaching concerning Jesus Christ. Peter stood and openly charged Caiaphas with the murder of Jesus Christ. Surely the high priest wanted to stop Peter and John just as much as he had wanted to stop Christ. However, he neither beat them nor crucified them. Instead, he threatened them and let them go "because of the people" (Acts 4:21).

You can be sure of this: if the multitudes had voiced themselves that Thursday night in Christ's behalf, Caiaphas might have once again altered his course. But this did not happen. That fateful Friday Jesus Christ was brutally cut down. After he had been scourged, mocked, and falsely accused, Jesus went to his death defense-less.

The Presence of Extremes

What happened? It seems that the streets of Jerusalem would have been crowded with people saying, "Look what he did for my baby; look what he did for my legs; look what he did to my eyes. He befriended me; he helped me." You don't forget a man who befriends you, much less saves your life. It seems someone would have insisted on giving a character witness in Christ's behalf. However, apart from a few weeping women, an over-whelming silence surrounded the cross of Jesus Christ—at least as far as the multitude was concerned. Is there any explanation for this silence?

Keep in mind that the whole plot was carefully planned. As mentioned above, the time and place were planned to avoid many of the people. However, the most careful planning was given to the scene before Pilate. The false accusation made against Christ worked in both directions. It helped frustrate Pilate. It also helped silence the people.

The Jewish authorities did not merely accuse Christ of trying to be a king. They said he was trying to set himself as a king in competition with the emperor, that he was trying to overthrow the government. Suddenly there was a problem of the presence of extremes. In truth, Jesus Christ did set himself up as a king. But he did not make claim to the extreme kingship the chief priests were forcing upon him. Pilate asked him, "Are you a king?" Christ refused to say no. He would not dignify the occasion with a last-minute explanation of his kingship.

The people did not know what to do. How could they say they believed Christ was a king without being accused of aiding in the overthrow of Rome? The word "king" had too many explosive meanings. Therefore, in the face of extremes, the people chose silence.

Contemporary Extremes

The presence of extremes has a way of silencing an individual. Recently I spoke with a friend who holds a high office in our state. He explained to me his personal dilemma. He said, "I do not enter into religious activities openly, and I have my reasons. On the one hand, I cannot identify with the wickedness, skepticism, and ungodliness in the world I serve daily. On the other hand, I cannot identify with the self-righteousness, piosity, and hypocrisy I find among certain people in the church. Therefore, in the face of these opposite frustrations, I simply make no comment at all on the subject of religion."

As we continued to talk he told me of his religious past. He gave testimony to what God had done for him, both past and present. He opened his heart to what God meant to him. He pulled a handkerchief from his pocket and wiped his eyes. We were both visibly moved. I realized I was standing before a deeply religious man. Yet, in the faces of extremes, he had not sought a mediating position for himself. Instead, he had chosen silence.

Extremes have a way of bringing silence, especially to the voices of good. The race tension has done this for us in our country. It has presented us with the problem of extremes. In a sense, we can thank the news media for the consistent exaggeration of extremes. Newsmen thrive on taking one radical viewpoint and contrasting it with an opposite view equally as radical. Any reporter would rather pit the Ku Klux Klan against a liberal, bearded, beatnik group of demonstrators. This makes good print. Such contrasts become the content for America's daily reading.

In the face of such extremes, each of us has had to ask these questions: "What is my responsibility to the problems of my day? Is there any word I should offer to the revolution in my society? Do I say or do anything? Or, in the face of extremes, is it my prime responsibility to remain silent?" If you have not asked yourself such questions, you should begin.

As a preacher I have asked myself, "What is my responsibility?" Most of us as ministers have been told repeatedly by members of our congregations, and other "interested friends," exactly what our position should be. We have been told we should say nothing; that we only fan the flames and add to the problem.

Recently a friend of mine met a bus driver from Tallahassee. My friend asked the gentleman if he knew C. A. Roberts. The bus driver replied, not too enthusiastically, that he did. The person asked, "Don't you like Dr. Roberts?" The man answered, "Oh, he's fine when he keeps his mouth shut about the race issue and sticks to his own business."

What do you think that bus driver would consider to be my business? I think I know what he would say. I think he would have me turn to the Old Testament, find some ancient historical biblical truth, and preach it. The idea behind such thinking is that as long as a truth is both *religious* and *remote*, it is safe, but the moment a truth reveals contemporary value, the moment it begins to apply to the tension of the day, it becomes unsafe and falls out of the realm of the preacher's business.

A minister is perfectly free to mention Martin Luther in a sermon. The German reformer, who helped free men from a different kind of slavery, is gone. He is buried beneath 450 years of history and, therefore, is safe to mention. But a minister dare not refer to Martin Luther King, for he is contemporary, and his name sets up extremes. I think the philosophy of the bus driver would be this: in the face of extremes, silence is golden. The best thing to say is nothing.

In the spring of 1965, Mark Van Doren brought the premier of his play, *Never Never Ask His Name,* to Tallahassee. It was a play of extremes; two men hating each other through ten years of silence and misunderstanding. The main theme of the play was that, in the face of misunderstanding, silence is never golden, but only *fool's gold!*

The same is true for our day. In the face of extremes, silence is idiotic; silence is confusing and leads to chaos.

For you can count on the fact that evil men are not going to remain silent. They never have and they never will! Evil men are going to talk and talk and talk. And, if good men remain silent, only one side will be heard. The end result is that good men suffer needlessly, and innocent men die.

Contemporary Silence

If the multitude at the trial of Jesus had only realized they didn't have to get into the political side of the issue; they did not have to tackle the problem of Christ's kingship. They could have rather said, with conviction, the things they knew in their hearts to be right. They could have risen up to say, "He is good, he is kind, compassionate, and loving. He is not trying to overthrow the government. He does not deserve to die!"

But the multitude remained silent. And I will always believe this is what hurt Christ most at the cross: not the brutality of the soldiers, not the accusations of Caiaphas, but the fact that those whom he loved, and who loved him, said absolutely nothing. They let him die defenseless. Surely any word would have been better than none.

I must admit that the philosophy of silence haunts me more than any of the previous ones we have mentioned. Have I ever known, as Simon did, an early commitment which I was later tempted to desert when it was no longer popular? I have to answer, *"guilty."* Like Judas, have I ever made a religious commitment on Sunday, only to be dominated by secular interests through the week? Again I have to plead *guilty*. Like Pilate, have I ever ignored what I knew in my heart was right, in order to protect myself? Guilty!

Yet, in my own life, I think I know which philosophy affects me most. If I could project myself back into the crucifixion scene, I think I know where I might have been. I do not think I would have been at the fire with Peter. I would not have been in the garden with Judas, nor at the palace with Caiaphas, nor at the court with Pilate. I am afraid I would have been somewhere milling in the crowd, loving Christ, hating what they were doing to him, but saying nothing!

What makes me reach this conclusion? Because I know what my response has been in many situations in the past. I have been where the name and spirit of Christ were being brought into ill repute. I have been where the attitudes that crucified Christ were operating. I have been where a witness was needed and called for, and I said nothing.

I challenge you to examine yourself. How many times have you been where men were crucifying the principles Christ died for? How often have you been where a witness was needed and called for, and you said nothing? This is what crucified Jesus Christ: not the *violence* of the evil ones, but the *silence* of the good.

The Challenge to Speak

Out of World War II came an incident in France. Boys from a neutral section were facing a choice as to which side they would cast their allegiance. One woman had two sons who kept delaying their decisions. She kept urging them to act, but to no avail. One morning she took her cloak and started out the door. The boys asked where she was going. The mother replied she was going to help in the war. The sons, argued, "But, Mother, you can't do any good." She replied, "Maybe not. But at least they will know which side I am on."

It is too late for me to undo my mistakes of the past, but there is one thing certain in my mind: Jesus Christ means all the world to me. I cannot believe in him and fail to try and imitate him. If it is possible, in the smallest way, to work his spirit through my life into society, I must try. Everything good I have received in life has come from him. All the hope, purpose, and promise I have for the future is wrapped up in him. As long as I have breath in my body, men must know which side I'm on.

Every time I am in a position where a witness for Christ is called for, in his name and in his spirit, I must try and give it. Where there is wrong, I must seek to correct it. And when I am wrong, I must try and change. I cannot let evil men around me, in the name of extremes, rip and tear my society, and myself contribute absolutely nothing. For not by the deeds of violence, but by the sin of silence, was our Lord finally nailed to a cross.

VI

The Way of Jesus—
GOODNESS AND REDEMPTION

> *I lay down my life*
>   *That I might take it again.*
> *No man taketh it from me,*
>   *But I lay it down of myself.*
> *I have the power to lay it down*
>   *And I have power to take it again.*
> *This commandment have I received*
>   *Of my Father.*
>
> JOHN 10:17–18

In previous chapters we have discussed philosophies that led to the cross. We examined the thought processes of men and groups that contributed to the act of putting Jesus Christ to death. We have looked at the cowardice of Peter, the materialism of Judas, the religion of Caiaphas, the ambition of Pilate, and the silence of the multitude.

The story of the crucifixion cannot be closed apart from one final philosophy—that of Jesus Christ himself. For although other attitudes and actions aided in Christ's death, none of them actually *caused* the crucifixion. The death of Jesus Christ was ultimately and actually brought about by the plan of God. Prior to the cross, Jesus Christ gave sole credit for his death to the plan of the Father (John 10:17-18). Therefore, we shall examine the philosophy of Jesus which led to the cross.

When we seek to uncover the philosophy of Jesus, we are immediately faced with a problem. Jesus Christ was both human and divine—both God and man. Because of this, we are not faced with one philosophy, but two. To be true to the paradox of Christ's nature, or person, we must take two separate approaches to the way of thinking which directed his actions. We must look at the philosophy which directed his daily actions on the human level. We must then look at the philosophy which represented the ultimate plan of God on the plane of the divine. Yet, we must keep in mind that these were not two separate philosophies, but one—and herein is the paradox. They were completely inseparable in the person of Christ. They merged to bring the climax of the crucifixion.

Human Goodness

In the difficult search for a word to represent the philosophy of Jesus on the human side, I have chosen the word "goodness." In the annals of significant men, the greater the man, the fewer words it takes to describe him. Luke gave possibly the clearest and most meaningful biography of Jesus from the human perspective when he said, "How God anointed Jesus of Nazareth with the Holy Ghost and with power: who went about doing good" (Acts 10:38).

From the beginning Jesus was not rejected because he was *bad*, but because he was *good*. Jesus had an uncompromising attitude toward truth. He had a supreme allegiance and devotion to rightness, or righteousness. The goodness of Jesus was *active*. It was always kept in the front of every discussion. He was always measuring people. He was continually confronting people with his brand of goodness, or godliness. He was so forceful and consistent that every person he met was spontaneously either drawn or repelled by his brand of goodness.

An interesting trend developed regarding the people Jesus met. He drew the people he should have repelled, and repelled the people he should have drawn. Look at the ones Christ drew to him. Were they of the religious set? Just the opposite. The "down-and-outers"—harlots, publicans, and sinners—were drawn to Christ. The "up-and-outers"—aristocratic businessmen, the wealthy wicked—were drawn to Christ. What caused this? Part of the answer lies in the fact that Christ would not tolerate inconsistency. Everywhere he found it, he exposed it. He offered a sense of respect to the man who could see himself as he was. He had no patience with superficiality.

There was one characteristic about the sinful set which surrounded Jesus. They were wicked, but they were honestly wicked. They were open about their plight in life. Consequently, Jesus was attracted to them, and they to him. He could deal with such men openly. He did not have to waste time or words cutting away a veil of pretense. Those who made up the sinful set were honestly convinced they were bad and, therefore, honestly admired the goodness of Christ.

With the religious set, the case was just the opposite. Here were men who daily paraded under robes of right-eousness. From the first day Christ met them, he gave them the title, "hypocrites." He saw their inconsistencies. He knew what they were pretending to be before men. He also knew what they really were on the inside. This inconsistency had a passionate reaction upon Christ, and he did not attempt to hide his feelings.

Among the religious leaders of the Jews, Jesus faced this group of hypocrites. These were not good men who were occasionally bad, but self-righteous men who pretended to be good. Jesus found a group of religionists who had built their lives on pretense, and he stripped it away. This is what initiated his rejection. It is true that the final debate resolved itself around theological issues regarding Christ's mission. What else would you have expected? But the fact remains that the goodness of Christ became a threat to Jewish hypocrisy. For three years his brand of goodness cut against the grain of pharisaical attitudes and actions. Therefore, it was not because of his badness (there was none), but because of his goodness, that Jesus was met with violent rejection.

Continuing Crucifixions

A few years ago, the best foreign film award was given to a religious film, *He Who Must Die*. The story

centered around a Greek Orthodox community during the
reign of the Turks. Each year the citizens enacted the
passion of Christ. They would choose the actors from
among themselves. The town elected a young man to
portray Christ because he seemed to be the one person in
the village who was completely without guile. The boy
and his fellow "disciples" were given six weeks to prepare
themselves spiritually.

In the meantime, a crisis arose involving a starving
neighboring community. Feeling his "elected" responsibility, the young man responded to the real life crisis with
what he was convinced was the pattern of Christ. Ultimately the boy was put to death at the hands of those who
had chosen him to play the role of Christ. The theme of
the story was this: there is inherent within the attitudes
and actions of men in every age, that which would crucify
the kind of goodness Jesus Christ brought to earth.

This is the message I have hoped to convey through
the pages of this book. Although twenty centuries have
passed since Christ was on earth, human nature has remained the same. The philosophies of cowardice, materialism, religious precedent, ambition, and silence are
just as alive as ever. Of one fact there can be no question.
If Christ were to come to any community in America
today, if he were to come incognito and assume the
position of an ordinary citizen, and if he were to bring his
brand of goodness to bear upon our society—we would
not tolerate his presence in our midst. We might not nail
him to a cross, but we would get him out of our town.

You say: "Not us, for we are civilized. We believe in letting a man have his place." Don't forget what I said earlier about the goodness of Christ. It was an *active* kind of goodness. He did not merely go around setting a good example for others to follow. He became a threat to the people around him. He not only called the names of sins, he also called the names of sinners! He would take a man's secret and shout it from the housetops. Men had to get rid of him for fear of being exposed for what they were. If Christ were here today, he would bring the same piercing, confronting, exposing type of goodness. We would not bear it. We would be rid of him in self-defense.

He Is Here

The above has been negative in its application. But there is also a positive challenge to the same truth. The Scriptures remind us that *Jesus Christ is here;* and I do not simply mean in the Spirit. The Bible states emphatically that Christians are to become the incarnation of Christ before the world. Christ promised to leave the world bodily, in order to return spiritually. He did not mean he would return to the world in general. Rather he promised to return to the hearts and lives of believers. Among his last words, Christ made a statement which should have a convincing impact upon us today. "If ye were of the world, the world would love his own: but because you are not of the world, but I have chosen you out of the world, therefore the world hateth you. Remember the word that I said unto you, The servant is not greater than his lord. If they have persecuted me, they will also persecute you" (John 15:19–20). A Christian who lets Christ live through him can expect the same treatment Christ received when he was on the earth.

Let me ask you a question. Has it been a fairly easy thing for you to represent Christ in your world? If so, it may be that you have accepted Jesus Christ, but rejected his righteousness! Occasionally a young person says, "I want to be true to God. But what if my friends ridicule me because of my witness for Christ?" Or a man says, "I want to be pleasing to God. But what if my associates reject me because of my Christian stand?" I always reply, "My friend, you better be concerned if they never ridicule, or if they never reject you." Jesus said one way you can know you belong to him is that you become his representative. The world rejected him; it will also reject you. The person who bears the goodness of Christ will walk a path that leads to a cross. A crossless Christianity is a Christless Christianity. It's as simple as that.

Divine Redemption

We have come now to that one pinnacle philosophy which actually *caused* the cross—the philosophy of redemption. Jesus died to redeem that which was lost. He did not die by accident. He did not die because things got out of hand. He did not die because of the action or thinking of any one person or group. Jesus died because it was the plan of God for him to die. Listen to his word, spoken many months prior to his crucifixion. "From that time forth began Jesus to shew unto his disciples, how that he must go unto Jerusalem, and suffer many things of the elders and chief priests and scribes, and be killed, and be raised again the third day" (Matt. 16:21). He did not imply that if he went to Jerusalem he might be killed. Rather he said that he must go to Jerusalem *in order to be killed.*

Examine carefully another passage. "I am the good shepherd: the good shepherd giveth his life for the sheep" (John 10:11). Also, "Therefore doth my Father love me, because I lay down my life, that I might take it again. No man taketh it from me, but I lay it down of myself" (vv. 17–18). Herein is the philosophy of redemption. Jesus did not die because of himself, but in behalf of others.

Interestingly enough, one of the clearest interpretations of redemption came from the enemies of Christ. First they nailed him to the cross. Then they walked beneath the cross and shouted, "He saved others; himself he cannot save" (Mark 15:31). In one sense, they told the truth, for he saved others by not saving himself.

Was there any reason, personal to himself, why Christ had to die? The answer is no. Could he have averted his death? The answer is yes. Could he have stopped the people from crucifying him? Yes! Listen to his words: "Thinkest thou that I cannot now pray to my Father, and he shall presently give me more than twelve legions of angels? But how then shall the scriptures be fulfilled, that thus it must be?" (Matt. 26:53–54). Could he have come down from the cross? Yes.

But—if he was going to save others, he had to do it by not saving himself. He could not save himself and redeem you and me. He chose us, and gave himself. He walked the earth as the sinless, innocent son of God. He drew to his breast all the sinful philosophies of men and bore them to a cross. He said, "Father, forgive them; for they know not what they do" (Luke 23:34). In this act, God said to you and me, "I love you, despite your sin; I love you regardless; my love is yours."

This is the philosophy of redemption. "Scarcely for a righteous man will one die: yet peradventure for a good man some would even dare to die. But God commendeth his love toward us, in that, while we were yet sinners, Christ died for us" (Rom. 5:7–8).

A Concluding Question

Our study up to this point will surely evoke one final series of questions. What if someone had spoken up? What if one of the principle figures leading to the cross had altered his action? What if Peter had not been a coward, or Pilate ambitious, or the crowd silent? Would any of this have stopped the crucifixion? The answer is no, for the cross was in the plan of God. Then another might ask, "What good, then, would it have done to speak?"

A hundred years ago a Negro killed an entire family in New York. He mercilessly slaughtered a father, mother, and children. The town wanted to lynch the man, but he was spared for a trial. However, no lawyer could be found who would defend him.

A young unknown lawyer, named Will Seward, went by to interview the defendant. He concluded the man was out of his mind, and had been at the time of the crime. He consented to be the lawyer for the defense. All through the trial young Seward persistently pleaded insanity for his client, but the jury had prejudged the defendant. In their minds, the man must die, and they returned a verdict of guilty. The Negro was quickly executed.

After the execution a postmortem was performed on the deceased. Upon examining his brain, the doctors concluded the Negro had been hopelessly demented. The man could not be brought back to life. However, because of his courageous stand, Will Seward came out of political obscurity and rose to Secretary of State under Lincoln.

I have not tried to infer that the actions or open defense of any one person would have stopped the crucifixion. But I am convinced of this: if one other disciple had stepped from the shadows to defend his Lord, his name would have lived in the hearts of believers in the centuries to come. And his example would have lent courage to future fearful, timid, silent followers who name the name of Christ.

Why John?

We would not be true to the account if we did not mention the one disciple who did follow Christ all the way to the cross. We have nothing that John said, only that he was there. I have asked myself many times, why John? Why was it that God let this one disciple live to be almost one hundred years of age? Why was it that he was the only one of the remaining eleven who did not die a martyr's death? Why was it that he was entrusted with the care of the mother of the Lord? Why was it that he was allowed to write the most significant Gospel? Why was it that he was given that mysterious vision called the Revelation?

The answer to these questions rests with God alone. But this I do know: there is one fact for which I remember John most, above all his other contributions; it was he who stood by the Lord to the end!

This is all God expects of any of his followers. We have the mistaken idea that God has called us to get results. We reason, "I know I should do this, or that—but after all, it wouldn't do any good."

Christian friend, God has not called any of his followers to get results, but rather *to be faithful!* And someday when we stand before him, we will not be called upon to list our victories, but to show wherein we were faithful! I believe if Jesus Christ were speaking today, he would not change his words: "Whosoever therefore shall be ashamed of me and of my words in this adulterous and sinful generation; of him also shall the Son of man be ashamed, when he cometh in the glory of his Father with the holy angels" (Mark 8:38).

VII

This Way
TO THE CROSS

A crossless Christianity
Is a costless Christianity
And a costless Christianity
Is a Christless Christianity

The crucifixion of Christ is history, but the race, for the Christian, goes on. He cannot turn back time, nor can he hide from the shadow of the crossed wood. He must rather let it fall upon him—and find his "way," through the "ways," to the light of God's favor.

Finding the way of Christ in a confused day like our own is no small task, for ours is a day of subtle and conflicting alternatives. If today's Christian will walk the way of Christ, he must first know where he stands in our split-level society.

I always wanted to live in a two-story house. There is something enchanting about a house with two distinct levels. The most appealing factor about such an arrangement is the distinct division between the two levels.

I recall entering a two-story house one day. Everything on the lower floor was immaculate and in its place. The second floor was a different matter. Things were out of place. Clothes were thrown around. There was the mark of extremely casual living. It was easy to tell which floor you were on simply by looking around.

Two-story houses today are no longer in vogue. They have given way to what architects call the split-level home. You enter the front door on a ground level. You take one step down to enter the living room. Two steps up and you are in the den. Three steps down and you are in the kitchen. One step up and you are in the hall. When you leave the house you feel as though you have walked through a four-story mansion. Once outside you look again to see only one floor with subtly split levels.

The American scene today could well be described as a split-level society. To understand what I mean, let me digress to the days when we had a two-story society.

The Two-Story Days

There was a time, not too many years ago, when men had far less trouble telling right from wrong.

Let me illustrate.

There was a day when most thinking men agreed that gambling was an extremely unhealthy practice. Shortly after coming to Florida I was privileged to eat dinner in the home of the honorable Doyle Carlton. Governor Carlton was in office during the days of the depression in the early thirties.

One day a group of men came to the governor's office. They placed on his desk a bag containing an enormous sum of money. They said it was his if he would sign the horse racing bill into law. The governor told the men they knew they were wasting their time, that such a bill would never become law while he was in office.

It did not, but that was back in a two-story day of the past. Today, Florida offers horse racing as one of its chief tourist attractions.

Do you remember the two-story days relating to beverage alcohol? There was a day when we knew that alcoholic beverage was a killer. It would eat away your stomach. It would eat away your brain. It would eat away your liver, your nerves, your home, and your job.

But that was before we learned that taxation could change the essential rightness of a thing.

I once heard the story of a donkey who was having his troubles. Mosquitoes were trying to get his blood. Occasionally he would kill one with the swish of his tail. One day a committee of mosquitoes came to the donkey with a bargain. Their spokesman said, "Let us take the blood we want. And everytime we take a quart, we will give you a pint in return."

He agreed. In a few days he was dead. You might expect a stupid donkey to fall for such a trick, but not sensible people.

And we didn't, back in the two-story days.

What ever happened to the good old American two-story attitude toward sex? Modesty, chastity and virtue used to be prized possessions in a girl's storehouse of character. Today I have a hard time finding teen-agers who have heard the words often enough to know what they really mean.

Let me mention a change I have noticed in the last ten years. Girls once would come to my study for counsel and *lie about their goodness.* They tried to make people believe they were better than they really were. Today the problem has reversed itself. Girls come and *lie about their badness.* They try to make people think they are worse than they really are. They are afraid they will be branded as virtuous and lose a degree of popularity. The irony is that boys have not changed in their attitude toward girls. They still think more of girls who think more of themselves.

There once was a two-story day of truth. A lie was something not true. There was no place for a white lie, or a necessary lie, or a half truth. A man's word actually was his bond. Today each man needs two lawyers: one to watch the other man, one to watch the other lawyer.

What about the two-story days of honesty? A cheat was a low, despicable character. Kids who cheated did so with a trembling conscience. Honesty was the best policy.

The problem today is this: honesty just does not seem to be the best policy. Why? Because we have brought right so far down and we have lifted wrong so far up that we really do not know which level is which.

The Split-Level Scene

In the light of the two-story past, let me point out the predicament of the split-level present.

Television scandals: A few years back we had an exposé of payola quiz programs. Contestants were getting the answers along with the questions. I questioned the people of my church. I could get no consensus about the essential wrongness of this practice. Here were some of the replies I received: "After all, it's just entertainment." "If you don't like it you can switch channels."

There was a hung jury regarding any real violation of ethics.

Athletics: Then came the point-shaving in major athletics. Every athlete knew it was wrong to lose a game intentionally, but the gambling syndicate tried a new procedure. They would say to a boy, "We don't want you to lose the game. We want you to win. We just want you to win by ten points instead of twenty."

Many frustrated athletes found themselves in an ethical twilight zone.

Industry: Then came the bid-letting scandals. This time major businessmen were infected. They were fine upstanding men in the community, leaders in their churches, men who would not think of robbing a bank or putting a gun in another man's back. Yet these same men began to meet together in hotel rooms. One would say, "You get the bid this time, and I'll get it next. That way we will not have to fight the problem of competitive bidding."

Check the number of reputable businessmen who have spent a year in jail in the last decade.

Medicine: Then came the insurance gimmick among physicians. This is so delicate I hesitate to mention it. A few years back I was talking to a doctor about the price of a forthcoming operation on my oldest daughter. He asked, "Do you have insurance?" I thought to myself: Does that mean if I don't have insurance he is going to charge me less? Or does it mean he is going to charge me what he should have charged in the first place?

I suppose your answer depends on whether you have a relative who is a physician.

Politics: Of course, we say jokingly, right and wrong is easier to determine in politics than anywhere else. It simply depends on whether you are a Democrat or a Republican, or whether you are a liberal or a conservative.

In the last major election we all noticed an interesting thing. Two opposing groups faced each other. Each was parading under the same banners of right, God, patriotism, honor, and truth. Each was pointing an accusing finger at the other and saying, "You are wrong."

Law: The legal profession has felt the thrust of the split-level ethic. A few years back the book, *Twilight of Honor,* was a best seller. The book got its title from some advice an older lawyer was giving to a younger man in his profession. He told him that a good lawyer had to have two souls. He had to have an ideal soul for the courtroom. He must defend right with all the fervor of his being in the courtroom, but he could not take his idealism out of the courtroom and try to force it on the society in which he lived. If he did he would slip into a twilight of honor and cut his own throat.

What was he saying? Very simply, that we no longer live in a society where people will tolerate a two-story attitude of right and wrong. The only thing that counts in our day is a man's political, economic, and social survival. Such self-preservation demands a split-level attitude toward ethics.

I was never so offended as when I first read Jean Paul Sartre's play, "The Respectable Prostitute." The setting is a small American community. The son of a state senator shoots and kills a Negro. The only witness is a prostitute. Another Negro is falsely blamed for the crime. The leadership of the town comes to the girl privately and tries to get her to forget what she saw. Here is a woman of ill repute who feels she ought to tell the truth, yet the respectable people of the town are trying to bribe her to lie.

I said it offended me when I first read it. I can no longer be offended. Not after the fall of 1964. Not after what happened in a community two hundred miles from my own town.

Two men confessed that they shot and killed a Negro, then they retracted their confessions. A third man stated that the two had, in fact, committed the crime. Later, he, too, retracted his statement. And the jury let the two men off scot free!

I say the judgment does not rest with those two men, nor with that jury, nor with that judge. The judgment rests with our whole society. North, south, east, west, we are sick!

Such a move to a split-level attitude toward ethics is not made without loss. We have suffered greatly in several areas.

What Have We Lost?

1. *We have lost our sense of direction.* Recently a boy tried to break the record in depth diving in Miami, Florida. With nothing but a small oxygen tank and a communications set, he went down into the sea. After he had broken the record, he sent word he was coming up, but he never did. Evidently the boy became confused by the sameness of his surroundings. He made the mistake of thinking that down was up and he plunged beyond a point of no return.

This has happened on the American scene. We have chipped away subtly and steadily at a solid view of ethics. We have come to a point where we think down is up, backward is forward, and wrong is right. We are fast approaching the point of no return.

2. *We have lost our fear of God.* There is a strange myth which we have swallowed as Americans. It is the fable that our country is so special in the eyes of God that he will protect us regardless of whether we are right or wrong. Did it ever occur to us that the men who wrote the Bible never knew there would ever be a country called the United States of America? If we were special, *they* did not know it.

Yet there is a truth that is written into every book in the Bible. God will never let a nation, or a community, or an individual *take a wrong road and reach a right destination*. This part of God's word seems to have little effect on our dulled sense of fear.

In the year 1900, Galveston, Texas, had never had a hurricane. The United States Weather Bureau sent word that one was coming. They urged the people to evacuate the island which was joined to the mainland by one iron bridge. Those who lived on the mainland took heed, but the residents of Galveston went out and looked at the sky. It was calm. Only a gentle breeze was blowing. Indifferently, they went to their beds.

During the night the gentle breeze became a strong wind. The strong wind brought a tidal wave which broke the bridge like a twig. The next morning the city of Galveston was virtually gone!

We, as Americans, refuse to heed the immutable warnings of God's word. We are basking in the gentle breezes of prosperity, but one day the gentle breeze will be gone, and with it will go a nation that has lost its fear of God.

3. *We have lost our sensitivity.* Probably our greatest loss lies in our inability to take a fair estimate of ourselves. I have no trouble seeing your faults, and you have no trouble seeing mine, but it is most difficult for either of us to see the error of his own way.

Here is the depressing truth in a nutshell. If you have read this book to this point, the odds are that you will not apply its message to yourself. You may see the plight of the other man. You may question the hidden prejudices of the author. Very few will say: "Oh, God, has this happened to me? Have I in any way lost my own perspective about the way of life that is right?"

Which Way to the Cross?

We have narrowed our questions to the one central theme: How does a man in a confused day like our own—one of conflicting interests and alternatives—find his way to the cross?

The answer was once simpler than it is today. The evangelist came to town and announced, "Return to Christ." That seemed to be sufficient. Today it is not enough, for we have made the same mistake that others made in other days. We have used the name of Christ but plotted a course of our own.

Today we must call for a return to the righteousness of Christ. Then we must make certain exactly what this implies. To my own mind it means two things.

First, we must treat every event as though we were Christ. We must seek to put his life into ours, and not the other way around. "What would Jesus do?" has been often asked but seldom done. Even so, playing the role of Christ is only one side of the coin. In fact there can be an air of arrogance in the attitude "What would Jesus do?" We can fall into the trap of doing what we think is best in the name of Christ. We must go on to the harder side of the righteousness of Christ—the side that is sorely lacking in our day.

Namely, we must treat every person as though he were

Christ. One day Jesus told a story of a group who were shut out of his kingdom. They could not understand why. He said: "*I* was hungry—not *they* were hungry—*I* was hungry and you did not feed me. I was naked and you did not clothe me. I was in prison and you did not visit me."

They replied, "When? When did we see you hungry and we did not feed you?"

Jesus replied: "Inasmuch as you did it not to the *least of these*, you did it not to me." Jesus stated unequivocably that the real issues of life center around how men treat each other. God meets men in one place—where men meet each other.

Registration can be a harrowing experience when it involves 13,000 people; it was almost too much for one student at the university near our church.

The young girl, a spastic, came to the final registration station. She was told she had made a mistake. It was too late in the day to correct the error; she would have to wait until the next week. This meant the penalty of late registration.

In desperation the girl returned to her dorm. Her roommates noticed that she was upset, but they didn't try to find out why. They were frankly embarrassed by her condition and excluded her.

The girl went into the bathroom and took an entire bottle of tranquilizer tablets. Once the reaction set in, she panicked. Suddenly she thought of Austin Hollady, the Methodist student director whom she had met earlier that day. Austin had noticed her that day in the registration line and had talked with her momentarily. In that brief conversation he had reached out and touched a lonely life. His was the name she remembered.

She raced out of the dorm and over to the Methodist Student Union. Austin took her to the hospital and the girl was saved.

The irony of the story is this: one of the girl's roommates had asked the question earlier that week—a question I hear repeatedly—"Preacher, what can we do on campus to be more effective witnesses for Christ?"

"Inasmuch as you did it not to the least of these . . . you did it not to me."

It was strange that the ones to whom Christ spoke could not recall when their failures occurred, but that is the terrifying problem of finding the way of Christ in a time of confused alternatives.

If only Peter had known whom he was denying, or Judas whom he was betraying, or Caiaphas what that night would mean to him eternally . . .

You must look for Christ in every event, listen for his will in every instant. Some seemingly insignificant moment, he will whisper to your better self:

"This way to the Cross."